AMAZING RESCUES

EMMA HAHN

illustrated by Laurie Spencer

J. WESTON
WALCH
PUBLISHER
Portland, Maine

1   2   3   4   5   6   7   8   9   10

ISBN 0-8251-0-2860-9

Copyright © 1997
J. Weston Walch, Publisher
P.O. Box 658 • Portland, Maine 04104-0658

Printed in the United States of America

Contents

Introduction . . . . *v*

Danger in the Antarctic 1

Buster 9

"Black Moses" of the Underground Railroad 17

Escape from the *Adelaide* 25

Cher Ami 33

Dogsled Express 41

Alligator Attack 49

Women to the Rescue 57

Priscilla the Pig 65

Lifesaving Underwear 71

Faster Than a Speeding Bullet 77

Frozen Alive 83

Introduction

Throughout history, people have helped one another. Often they have performed superhuman deeds in dangerous, life-threatening situations. No one plans for these emergencies. Most often they occur without warning. And such disasters can strike very quickly. People can be hopelessly trapped by circumstances totally beyond their control.

The following 12 stories are all true. In each story, a person or an animal puts his or her own life at risk to rescue another from death, danger, or disease. These 12 acts of courage involve men, women, and children, an escaped slave, an explorer, a skydiver, a little dog, a 22-pound pig, a pigeon, and even a pair of long johns! Ordinary people, animals, and things responding to extraordinary circumstances.

After you read these stories, you may eventually forget the details of each dangerous situation. But you will remember how the people involved responded. You'll remember what they did to avoid tragedy.

To help you better understand each story, there are activities that follow. They will also help you imagine how you might rescue someone from a similar situation.

Danger in the Antarctic

Sir Ernest Henry Shackleton was no stranger to the Antarctic. As a young naval lieutenant, he went on the British National Antarctic (Discovery) Expedition from 1901 to 1904. Led by Captain Robert Falcon Scott, the expedition explored the continent, looking for the South Pole. The team discovered Edward VII Peninsula and surveyed the coast of Victoria Land.

In 1907 Shackleton returned to the Antarctic with his own British expedition on his ship *Nimrod*. The explorers climbed to the summit of Mount Erebus (12,448 feet), located at the southern magnetic pole, and trekked across ice and snow to get within 100 miles of the South Pole. When Shackleton returned to England two years later, he was knighted and made a companion of the Royal Victorian Order.

In 1914 he led the British Imperial Trans-Antarctic Expedition. This adventure nearly cost the lives of everyone in his party. The explorers hoped to be the first to cross Antarctica via the South Pole on foot. But they never reached their starting base on the Weddell Sea. Their ship *Endurance* got hemmed in by ice floes. It drifted off the coast for 10 months before being crushed in a pack of solid ice.

On December 15, 1915, Shackleton ordered his men to abandon the crushed ship. They were 200 miles from the nearest land, Elephant Island. And they were 1000 miles from the nearest humans. Dragging the ship's lifeboats, the 27 men set off on foot toward Elephant Island. Shackleton knew their chances of reaching the island were slim. So he left a note on board the *Endurance.* He wanted the world to know what had happened in case he and his men disappeared forever.

Trudging through slushy ice—sometimes sinking up to their knees—the men covered barely 10 miles in five days. Shackleton feared their strength would give out. He decided to make a camp on the biggest ice floe. "We'll wait here till the ice pack breaks up. Then we'll launch the lifeboats."

They lived in tents on top of the ice for five long months. Temperatures stayed well below zero. The winds were ferocious. There was no way to replenish the dwindling supply of food. The men were afraid the ice would carry them away from Elephant Island. The island was nothing but a giant rock. But it was their last hope. Beyond it stretched 3000 miles of open ocean.

The big floes began to break up in April. Still, Shackleton hesitated to launch the lifeboats. He feared the sharp edges of the huge ice splinters would stave in the sides of the boats.

Then the floe on which the men were camped suddenly split in two pieces. The men barely had time to jump onto the half with all their equipment before the other half floated away.

They launched the lifeboats. They soon found that life in the boats was much harsher than life on the ice floe. The wind increased over the open water. Thirty-foot waves threatened to swamp the boats. The men got coated with frozen spray. They ached from the cold and from the constant rowing.

They rowed for five days and nights. Finally they reached Elephant Island. Still, that wasn't the end. It was dry land. But there was no food on the island. Nothing grew on it. Ships had no reason to stop there.

Shackleton knew there were food and people on South Georgia Island. The problem was that South Georgia Island lay another 800 miles across the ocean. Shackleton knew he had to try to get there. He chose five men to come with him in the boat. The other 22 stayed behind on Elephant Island.

The men parted with little hope of ever seeing each other again. To reach South Georgia Island, Shackleton had to go around Cape Horn. That was considered to be the most dangerous stretch of ocean in the world.

The little boat barely made it around the horn. The men struggled against 80 mph winds and 50-foot waves. They were running out of food. And, even more important, they were running out of water. Finally they spotted some wood and seaweed. That meant land was close by. They landed at last. Then they had a 29-mile trek to Stromness, a village on the other side of the island.

It took them almost two weeks to cross the mountains into Stromness. Then, bad weather prevented ships from sailing back to Elephant Island to rescue the other explorers. After four unsuccessful attempts, Shackleton finally landed a ship on Elephant Island on August 30, 1916. Miraculously, all 22 of his men were still alive. Shackleton's long and grueling rescue efforts had paid off.

Activities

I. Recalling the Rescue

Answer the following questions to see how many details you can remember from the story.

1. What country was Shackleton from?

2. How did the explorers on Scott's expedition get around the Antarctic?

3. What was the name of the first ship Shackleton sailed to the Antarctic?

4. What mountain did the explorers climb? How tall was it?

5. What was the name of Shackleton's 1914 expedition?

6. How many months was the *Endurance* hemmed in by ice floes?

7. What was the name of the island closest to Shackleton's wrecked ship?

II. *If You Had Been in this Situation . . .*

1. Would you have abandoned your wrecked ship to find help? Why or why not?

2. If you had lost your compass in the wreck, how could you figure out in which direction you were walking across the ice?

3. What would have been your greatest fear as you set out on foot in the Antarctic?

III. *Vocabulary to the Rescue*

Locate the following words in the story. Make a new sentence about an amazing rescue adventure for each.

- stranger

- dogsled

- expedition

- explorers

- hemmed in

- abandon

- dwindling

- swamp

- grueling

- ice splinters

Buster

Buster was a small black-and-tan Spitz dog. He lived with his family, Mr. and Mrs. Remackels and their Persian cat named Fluffy. They lived in an apartment house in Minneapolis, Minnesota.

Fluffy had attached herself to Buster from the day he saved her life. When Fluffy was just a tiny kitten, she wandered into the woods behind the Remackels's apartment house. There, she caught her front paw in a small animal trap. Buster heard her mewing and went into the woods and found her. He gently grabbed the scruff of her neck with his mouth and carried Fluffy— trap and all—back home. As soon as Mrs. Remackels freed her from the trap, Fluffy attached herself to Buster like his shadow. Night and day, she was always at his side.

So, it was not at all unusual to find them sleeping in the same corner of the house, as they were on April 13, 1930. At 4 o'clock that morning, Buster woke up in a cloud of thick smoke. He sensed something was terribly wrong. He nudged Fluffy awake. Then he dashed down the hall to the Remackels's bedroom.

Buster pushed his way in through the bedroom door. He put his front paws up on the pillow and licked Mrs. Remackels's face. She tried to push him away. He barked and jumped up on the bed. Still not aware of the dense smoke, Mrs. Remackels started to pull the covers up over her head to get away from Buster. But Buster grabbed her arm in his mouth and firmly clamped his teeth around it.

"Ouch! That's too rough," said Mrs. Remackels as she tried to push Buster away.

But Buster wouldn't let go. He knew he had to get her up no matter what.

"Okay, okay," Mrs. Remackels started to say before she was struck with a fit of coughing. Suddenly she realized the room was full of smoke. She could hardly breathe. She grabbed Mr. Remackels and shook him awake, too.

Buster kept tugging at their pajamas until they got out of bed. There was no time to stop for a coat or even a bathrobe. They couldn't see a thing through the thick smoke. They stumbled out of the bedroom and followed the sound of Buster's barking. He led them downstairs to the ground floor of their apartment building.

As soon as they were outside the building's front door, Buster raced back inside. He ran upstairs and down the hallway to the neighbor's apartment. There he barked as loud as he could and threw himself against the door. The sleepy tenant opened the door to see what all the racket was about.

Meanwhile Buster ran down the hall to the next door. Again he barked and hurled himself against the door. When he heard the people inside moving around, he went on.

Other neighbors woke from the commotion. Frightened families, half-asleep and half-dressed, stumbled and ran down the hall. They were desperate to get out of the smoky building.

At the last door, Buster couldn't get a response. He barked and scratched and threw himself against the door. But no one came to open it. Finally he ran down the hallway, stopped, turned, and then shot back toward the door at full speed. His small body hit with such force that the door broke open.

Buster tore inside. There he found a very old man in bed, almost unconscious. Buster jumped up on the man's chest. He licked his face, and barked right in his ear. Then Buster pulled at the covers. At last the man got up. He stumbled toward the door. Buster was right at his heels. Barking and nipping, Buster led the man outside. There the other tenants were huddled together across the street from the burning building.

Buster took a quick look at the crowd. Someone was missing. Buster dashed back into the now fiercely burning building. He could barely see, his eyes were watering so from the smoke. The floorboards were very hot on his little feet. Yet he kept going till he reached his own apartment.

Buster barked. Through the dense smoke, something staggered towards him. It was Fluffy. The kitten collapsed at his feet. Once again, Buster picked her up by the scruff of the neck and carried her to safety.

The fire destroyed the apartment house. But thanks to Buster's courage and quick thinking, 35 people and a kitten survived. Buster received a gold medal from the city for his amazing rescue effort.

Activities

I. Recalling the Rescue

Answer the following questions to see how many details you can remember from the story.

1. In what city did Buster live?

2. What kind of dog was Buster?

3. What color was Buster?

4. What kind of cat was Buster's friend Fluffy?

5. What time did the fire wake Buster up?

6. How did Buster wake up his neighbors?

7. How many people did Buster rescue?

8. Who was rescued last?

II. *If You Had Been in This Situation . . .*

1. What is the first thing you should do if a fire breaks out in your house or apartment?

2. Should you stand up and run through the smoke or crawl along the floor to get out of a burning building?

3. Would you run back into a fire to try to save a pet you love?

III. *Vocabulary to the Rescue*

Locate the following words in the story. Make a new sentence about an amazing rescue adventure for each.

- commotion

- wandered

- scruff

- shadow

- clamped

- fit

- racket

- frantically

- hurled

- unconscious

"Black Moses" of the Underground Railroad

Harriet Tubman was born in 1820 on a slave plantation in Bucktown, Maryland. She was one of 11 children. At the age of seven, she was sent into the fields to work with the other slaves.

Slaves were treated badly on the plantation owned by Edward Brodas. Harriet had been beaten many times. At age 13 she was hit on the head by an overseer when she refused to help him tie up another slave. Her skull was fractured. She lay unconscious for many weeks. But as soon as she was able to get up, she was sent right back into the fields.

Slaves lived in constant fear of being sold to other plantation owners. Brodas had sold two of Harriet's sisters. And he was planning to sell Harriet and her two brothers to another plantation in the deep South. But he died before he could carry out that plan.

The new master put Harriet to work with her father. Their job was cutting down trees to be shipped to the mills in Baltimore. In 1844 Harriet married another hand, John Tubman. Harriet could not read or write. But she heard stories about being free. She longed to find this thing called freedom.

Harriet's father realized that no one would prevent his daughter from trying to escape. He began to teach her ways to survive in the woods.

One night Harriet overheard the master talking about her. He said that she had been sold and would be leaving the plantation the next morning. Harriet knew she had to make her break before dawn. She tried to convince her husband to come, too. But he was afraid to try. In the middle of the night, Harriet escaped into the woods. Her two brothers escaped with her. They headed North.

Before long, her brothers became afraid and turned back to the plantation. So Harriet went on alone. She traveled by night and hid in the woods during the day. Finally she crossed the border into Pennsylvania—a state with no slavery. She was free! She said, "I looked at my hands to see if I was the same person . . . I felt like I was in heaven."

Harriet got a job as a cook. She earned money to spend. She could go where she wanted, as long as she stayed in the North. She would have been very happy, but she kept thinking about friends and family who were still slaves. She wanted to do something to help them.

A friend told her about the underground railroad. "It's not a train," he said. "It's special houses where slaves can hide during the day as they make their way along a route to the North. I've heard they need people to be conductors to help guide the slaves from house to house."

"I'll help," said Harriet.

"It's dangerous work," her friend warned.

That didn't bother Harriet. She was ready to risk her life to rescue others from slavery. In all she made 19 trips back into the South and rescued over 300 slaves, including many members of her own family.

Her reputation for bravery spread. Soon she was called Black Moses for helping so many slaves escape to freedom.

This made the slave owners furious. They decided to offer an award for her capture. A group collected enough money for a $40,000 reward. That was a huge amount of money then. They made a wanted poster with Harriet's picture on it. They posted it all over the South and in the border states.

Now it was even more dangerous for Harriet to go back and help slaves. But that didn't stop her. She didn't even stop in 1858 when the U.S. government passed the Fugitive Slave Law. This law made it legal for slave catchers to enter northern cities, capture runaway slaves, and return them to their owners. Harriet just kept going farther North. Sometimes she went all the way to the border of Canada. Later she said, "I never ran my train off the track and I never lost a passenger."

One day two men recognized her when she was riding south on a real train. She pulled the hood of her bonnet down over her face. She got off the train at the next stop. Just outside the station, she spotted her old master walking towards her.

She ducked into the village market. There she bought two live chickens. She tied their feet together, slung them over her arm, and continued walking down the street. As her old master drew closer, she untied the string and set the chickens free.

Flapping wildly, the chickens fell to the ground. Dust swirled as they squawked and sputtered and danced circles around everyone. The chickens created such a fuss, the old master never saw his escaped slave with the $40,000 price on her head.

When the Civil War began, Harriet volunteered to be a spy for the Union Army. One of her famous escapades was reported in the *Boston Commonwealth* newspaper: "On July 10, 1863, Colonel Montgomery and his gallant band of 300 black soldiers, under the guidance of a black woman, dashed into the enemy's country, struck a bold and effective blow, destroying millions of dollars of commissary stores, cotton and lordly dwellings, and rescued 800 slaves."

After the war she continued to come to her people's rescue. In 1908 she converted a house and 25 acres of land she had bought in Auburn, New York, into a home for orphans, the elderly, and former slaves with no place to go. She fed the people with money she earned selling fruit from her land and copies of a biography about her life.

Harriet Tubman died in 1913 at the age of 93. A hero to her people and her country, she was buried with full military honors.

Activities

I. Recalling the Rescue

Answer the following questions to see how many details you can remember from the story.

1. In what century was Harriet Tubman born?

2. What was the name of her first plantation master?

3. What kind of work did Harriet's father do on the plantation? How was it of help to her?

4. How did Harriet know she was about to be sold?

5. Did Harriet escape with her husband?

6. What was the name of the first free state Harriet escaped to?

7. How much of a reward were the slave owners willing to pay for Harriet's capture?

8. What was the Fugitive Slave Law?

II. If You Had Been in This Situation . . .

1. Would you have gone back to rescue others if you knew there was a big reward for anyone who could capture you?

2. What would you do to cause a distraction if there were no chickens at hand?

3. Would you be willing to hide someone in your house if you had to risk your own life to protect theirs?

III. *Vocabulary to the Rescue*

Locate the following words in the story. Make a new sentence about an amazing rescue adventure for each.

- slave

- plantation

- fractured

- unconscious

- escape

- dawn

- underground

- dangerous

- cook

- risk

Escape from the Adelaide

Off the New Jersey shore by Barnegat Light, the sloop *Adelaide* foundered. The weather on September 10, 1846, had changed suddenly. An offshore gale had blown up huge waves that were washing over the *Adelaide*'s deck.

On shore, lighthouse keeper John Allen and two men named Collins and Herring watched helplessly. There was nothing they could do to help. It happened fast. The boat capsized and the hull was dashed into a sandbar.

Allen and the other two men knew they couldn't get through the raging sea to the wreck. Even if they could have, it was surely hopeless. No one on board could have survived.

Hours later, waves drove the battered hulk—still bottom up—ashore. "It will be night soon," said Allen. "I've got to stay and light the lamp. You two try to get to the wreck and see if there's anything to be salvaged from it."

Collins and Herring struggled through the roaring wind and driving rain. The going was rough. But they had to get across the beach while the tide was still low. Pounding waves rocked the battered hull back and forth, burying it deeper in the sand.

Herring and Collins reached the wreck. They could barely see through the wind and water. They crawled on top of the slippery keel. The noise of the wind, the surf, and the sloop's timbers tearing apart was almost deafening.

But Herring heard something else. "Collins!" he shouted. "Something's knocking from inside."

Collins dragged himself over by Herring. But the knocking had stopped.

A beam shot across the water. "Allen's got the lamp lighted," yelled Herring.

"Yeah, and the tide is coming in mighty fast. We better get out of here while we can," Collins shouted back.

Just then, the mysterious knocking started again. Collins put his ear against the barnacle-covered hull. "I feel something pounding against the timbers," bellowed Collins.

"Someone or something is still alive in there," shouted Herring. "We need two axes and a lantern. Go quickly. We've little time to spare."

Collins went back to the lighthouse as fast as he could. The incoming tide lashed against his legs. Several times he was swept off his feet. Twenty minutes passed before he got back to the ship. He struggled on board with the gear. The tide was moving in with alarming speed.

"Good work," yelled Herring. "I think the knocking's coming from the main cabin. If we hurry, we stand a chance of rescuing whatever it is."

The two men managed to chop an opening in the thick hull. It was almost impossible for Herring to light the lantern in the wind. But he finally got it lighted. He thrust it inside the hole. "Try to hang on just a little longer," he shouted.

"I will," a voice came back.

"Well, I'll be!" yelled Herring. "It's a girl!"

The incoming tide was rapidly flooding the cabin. The men worked fast to enlarge the opening.

Giant waves crashed over them. But Herring and Collins didn't stop chopping. Then a tremendous wave knocked them off their feet. The water went into the hole. Then it shot back out in a huge spume.

"Just like a whale!" sputtered Herring as he half swam, half crawled back to look in the hold. "She's still alive," he started to yell at Collins. But he saw another enormous wave coming at them. "Give me your hands," he shouted into the hole.

Two tiny arms poked out of the opening. Herring grabbed hold of the wrists. The towering wave crashed over them. They were buried in swirling foam. But Herring never let go of the girl.

The wave receded. Herring quickly lifted the girl through the opening. Another gigantic waved loomed above. It took the combined strength of Herring and Collins to hold onto the girl and the hull at the same time. The thundering surge knocked their breath away.

"I thought we were goners for sure," said Collins as the water washed back.

Carrying the young girl, he and Herring half swam, half walked, ashore. Finally they reached the lighthouse. Allen bundled all three of them in blankets. And he gave them mugs of steaming cider.

The girl was dazed and frightened. She could not remember her name. But she did know that the *Adelaide*'s captain was her father. "After Mama died last month," she said, "Poppa thought a sea voyage might help both of us. When we ran into the gale, Poppa sent me below for safekeeping. I was alone in his cabin when the boat capsized. It was dark," she said. "Everything in the cabin whirled around me. I was terrified."

Miraculously the girl had been thrown into a corner that held a pocket of air. There she had clung to the floorboards. Hearing Herring and Collins above her, she had knocked.

She was the only survivor of the *Adelaide*. Her father and the crew had drowned when the boat capsized. The captain's daughter was raised by relatives. When she became of age, she married . . . a sailor!

Activities

I. Recalling the Rescue

Answer the following questions to see how many details you can remember from the story.

1. What time of year was the *Adelaide* wrecked?

2. On the shore of what state is Barnegat Lighthouse?

3. What kind of storm suddenly struck?

4. What happened to the boat?

5. What was the name of the lighthouse keeper?

6. Who first heard knocking from inside the wreck?

7. How did the captain's daughter survive when the *Adelaide* capsized?

8. How did Collins and Herring rescue the girl from the wrecked hull?

II. If You Had Been in This Situation . . .

1. How would you feel if you witnessed a shipwreck like this and had no way to help anyone on board the boat?

2. What would you do if you were trapped in an upside-down boat that was almost completely filled with water?

3. Can you think of any other way you could have gotten the captain's daughter out of the boat?

III. *Vocabulary to the Rescue*

Locate each of the following words in the story. Make a new sentence about an amazing rescue adventure for each.

- helplessly

- founder

- sandbar

- battered

- wreck

- deafening

- mysterious

- barnacle

- whirled

- gale

Cher Ami

Carrier pigeons were often used on the front lines in World War I. They carried messages between soldiers during battle. The messages were on tiny scraps of paper, rolled inside a small tube attached to the pigeon's leg.

The birds, of course, were specially trained. Cher Ami was an English pigeon donated to the American Army Signal Corps. He underwent his greatest test at the Battle of the Argonne in October 1918.

American armies were locked in fierce battle against enemy German troops. Cher Ami and four other caged carrier pigeons were carried into battle by American soldiers of the 308th Regiment.

These 700 men spearheaded the attack against the German soldiers. The pigeons were terrified by the gunfire and exploding artillery shells. They huddled together for comfort.

The Americans had advanced well into enemy territory when they received a message: "Do not advance any farther." Unfortunately the message came too late. The enthusiastic American company of soldiers had charged in fast and far ahead of the rest of the troops. The Germans had cut them off, surrounded them, and were pounding them with machine-gun and mortar fire.

The sergeant in charge of the pigeons released one of the five birds with a message requesting artillery aid. The pigeon did not make it across the battlefield. The sergeant released a second pigeon with the same message. It, too, was shot down by enemy gunfire.

The army was trapped for two days. Casualties ran high. Through some terrible miscalculation, behind-the-lines American artillery were firing on the trapped company of soldiers. Only 245 of the original 700 men remained.

Food and water were nearly gone. A third pigeon was launched. The troops were desperately trying to tell their own army to lift its fire. German sharpshooters brought the pigeon down immediately. The German commander demanded surrender. The Americans refused.

Now there were just two pigeons left. The fourth pigeon escaped from the soldier's grasp and flew away before the message was inserted in the leg tube. Cher Ami was the only carrier pigeon left—the soldiers' last hope.

The message was successfully inserted in the tube on Cher Ami's leg. The bird took off. He flew barely a hundred yards. Then he dove into a tree, taking refuge from enemy fire. A soldier risked his life to drive the bird out of hiding.

Cher Ami circled to determine the direction of home base. Finding it, he flew off through an incredible barrage of gunfire. He was struck in the head by a bullet that destroyed his left eye. Another bullet ripped into his chest. Remarkably, he continued flying home.

But his horrific flight was not over. A piece of shrapnel cut off his right leg. Still the brave bird kept flying—purely on instinct now. He made it home with the message still intact on his remaining leg. As soon as the soldiers learned they were shelling their own men, they stopped.

Once the "friendly" fire was lifted, the besieged company was able to fight its way out of the German army's trap.

Cher Ami recovered from his wounds, was awarded a medal for outstanding bravery, and was shipped back to the United States in a special "officer's" cabin on a naval warship.

Activities

I. Recalling the Rescue

Answer the following questions to see how many details you remember about the story.

1. What kind of bird was Cher Ami?

2. How did birds carry messages?

3. For which army was Cher Ami flying?

4. How many pigeons did the 308th Regiment originally carry into this battle?

5. Which countries are fighting in this story?

6. What happened to the fourth pigeon?

7. Where did Cher Ami try to hide?

8. What was the extent of Cher Ami's wounds?

II. If You Had Been in This Situation . . .

1. Would you have chased Cher Ami or let him hide?

2. Once you were trapped, would you have encouraged your men to surrender?

3. How would you have rewarded Cher Ami for his bravery?

III. Vocabulary to the Rescue

Locate each of the following words in the story. Make a new sentence about an amazing rescue adventure for each word.

- front lines

- battle

- combat

- enemy

- caged

- gunfire

- exploding

- besieged

- artillery

- casualties

Dogsled Express

In January 1925, a diphtheria epidemic struck the town of Nome, Alaska. Diphtheria is like an extremely bad cold that goes amok. It is a highly infectious, life-threatening disease. It creates a toxin or poison harmful to the heart and central nervous system. In 1925 nine out of every ten people who came down with diphtheria died.

There was a cure. A medicine called an antitoxin could stop the disease and keep it from spreading. But there was no antitoxin in Nome when Dr. Curtis Welch diagnosed his first case of diphtheria there.

Dr. Welch was worried because he knew the disease could kill all of the 1429 citizens of Nome. He asked town officials to close the school, the movie house, and other public gathering places where the germs could easily be spread.

The nearest supply of antitoxin was in Anchorage. That city was 900 miles away. Being the middle of winter, the roads between Anchorage and Nome were closed. The weather was too bad for airplanes to fly. And the nearest railroad station was 650 miles from Nome.

The people of Nome asked the governor for help. The governor decided the railroad would carry the antitoxin as far as possible. Then the medicine would be carried the last 650 miles by dogsled. It was the only way. Time was short.

Relay dog teams were set up to carry the antitoxin, just as the old Pony Express riders carried mail across the American West. About 20 teams and their mushers (drivers) were needed. Many mushers volunteered to help.

It was a brutal trip. Temperatures averaged about −50° F. Icy winds and snow made it very tough going. Still, one musher made his part of the journey even tougher.

Leonard Seppala knew every delay meant more people in Nome would die. So he decided to take a dangerous shortcut. Instead of going around Norton Bay, he went straight across the frozen water.

Seppala knew the risk. If the ice broke up, the 80 mph winds would sweep him, his team, and the valuable medicine into the water. He pushed ahead. It was a grueling stretch for him and the dogs. But they made it. They passed the antitoxin on to the next musher ahead of schedule.

The last musher was Gunnar Kasson. It was 8 o'clock at night when he received the antitoxin. It was out of the question to think of heading out in the dark. But Kasson knew that five more people had died in Nome. He hitched up his team.

They headed out. The weather grew worse. The bitter wind froze Kasson's right cheek. His hands became numb. Pieces of ice froze between the dogs' toes. The dogs' paws began to bleed.

The blinding snow confused Kasson. He lost the trail. Suddenly, he had no idea where they were. He could not see. Kasson called out to his lead dog, Balto. The dog was his only hope. Balto would have to try to pick up the scent of the trail.

Kasson knew it was a long shot. He wondered how any dog could sniff out a trail in the dark, in a blinding snowstorm, in the middle of the frozen wilderness.

Balto sniffed first in one direction, then another. He zigzagged back and forth. Finally he picked up a scent. He sped off with the team behind him. He had found the trail.

Balto led Kasson and the team, exhausted and half frozen, into Nome at 5:36 the next morning. The lives of many people of Nome were saved thanks to mushers like Kasson and Seppala and brave dogs like Balto.

Activities

I. Recalling the Rescue

Answer the following questions to see how many details you can remember from the story.

1. What kind of epidemic hit Nome?

2. Where is Nome?

3. What parts of the body does this disease attack?

4. Was there a cure for the disease?

5. Why did Dr. Welch close public places?

6. How close did the railroad come to Nome?

7. What was the dangerous shortcut that Seppala took?

8. How did Balto find the trail in the middle of the blinding snowstorm?

II. If You Had Been in This Situation . . .

1. Would you have driven your team across the frozen bay?

2. Could you think of a way to protect the sled dogs' paws from the ice and snow?

3. What would you do to make sure this kind of emergency never happened again?

III. *Vocabulary to the Rescue*

Locate each of the following words in the story. Make a new sentence about an amazing rescue adventure for each.

- epidemic

- amok

- infectious

- antitoxin

- germs

- delay

- shortcut

- grueling

- volunteered

- numb

Alligator Attack

They called it Lake Louise. But it wasn't a real lake. It was just a rock pit filled with water. It was located in an old quarry outside Coral Cables, Florida. Sometimes small fish like minnows were found in it. So kids liked to fish there.

On a hot September day in 1951, a nine-year old girl named Gerry Gustafson and her ten-year-old friend Parker Stratt went to the lake. They tried to scoop up minnows in their hands near the water's edge. They were so busy following the tiny fish that they did not see the seven-foot alligator in the water. The alligator was lurking under the surface of the lake.

Later, people said that the alligator must have been searching for food when it wandered into the quarry. There was little natural food in the pit to attract an alligator. So by the time it spotted Gerry, the alligator was probably hungry enough to attack anything that looked edible.

Without warning, the huge alligator shot out of the water and snapped its jaws around Gerry's arm. Gerry screamed. The sharp teeth closed like a vice. The creature dragged Gerry into the water, deeper and deeper. Suddenly, it opened its mouth. It may have just wanted to get a better grip. Gerry bobbed to the surface and thrashed her way toward shore.

Parker, too horrified to move at first, sprang into action. He grabbed the roots of a tree on the shore with one hand. Then he reached out for Gerry with the other hand. He caught one of her flailing arms. He tried to pull her in.

The alligator saw its meal escaping. It sped in, clamped its jaws around Gerry's legs, and tried to pull the girl back into deep water.

Gerry shrieked. She was caught in the middle of a life-and-death tug-of-war. The alligator was much stronger than the boy. And the boy had nothing—not even a stick or branch—to use for beating back the alligator. But Parker refused to let go of Gerry.

Then, once again, the alligator mysteriously released its grip. Parker didn't hesitate. He snatched Gerry out of the creature's reach. He half dragged, half carried Gerry over to his bike.

With wild anger, the alligator lunged out of the water. It raced after the children, snarling and snapping its jaws.

Somehow Parker got Gerry onto his bicycle. Together they rode to a nearby bus repair garage. As soon as the mechanics saw the children, they rushed up to help. They bandaged Gerry's badly torn arm and her leg wound, wrapped her in a blanket, and drove her to the hospital.

Gerry survived the alligator attack. The doctors were even able to save her badly wounded arm.

It was Parker, however, whose courage and quick thinking truly saved his friend's life. Parker was one of the first persons to receive the Young American Medal for Bravery for this amazing rescue. President Harry Truman awarded it to him in a special White House ceremony.

Years after the alligator incident, Parker became a lifeguard in South Miami. There he was called upon many times to save lives. Still, his most vivid lifesaving memories remained those of rescuing his friend Gerry from the jaws of death.

Activities

I. *Recalling the Rescue*

Answer the following questions to see how many details you can remember from the story.

1. Where was Lake Louise?

2. What kind of fish might be found in the lake?

3. Was Parker older or younger than Gerry?

4. What was the alligator doing in the quarry?

5. How big was the alligator?

6. What part of Gerry did the alligator bite first?

7. How did Parker get Gerry to the garage for help?

8. Which U.S. president awarded Parker the Young American Medal for Bravery?

II. If You Had Been in This Situation . . .

1. Would you have held onto Gerry or let go to try to find a branch or something to fight the alligator with?

2. How would you have carried Gerry on your bicycle? Or, if you do not have a bicycle, how would you have gotten help for Gerry?

3. How would you feel if the president of the United States wanted to meet you?

III. Vocabulary to the Rescue

Locate each of the following words in the story. Make a new sentence about an amazing rescue adventure for each.

- quarry

- alligator

- lurking

- hungry

- attack

- edible

- warning

- vice

- horrified

- flailing

Women to the Rescue

In the nineteenth century, two young women from opposite shores of the Atlantic Ocean became famous for their daring sea rescues.

Grace Darling was born in 1815 in a lighthouse. She was the seventh child of William and Thomasin Darling. William Darling was keeper of the Longstone Lighthouse in the Farne Islands off the coast of England.

The Darlings had nine children in all. The children lived and learned how to read and write in their seven-room lighthouse. Grace helped with the inside chores. But she loved it best when her father let her help row his boat. He had a short, flat-bottomed rowboat. He used the boat to travel between the islands.

When Grace was 22, a luxury steamboat named the *Forfarshire* was wrecked in a violent storm one night. High waves dashed the boat into the rocks. Forty-three people drowned immediately. Nine people escaped in a lifeboat. Grace and her father spotted nine others desperately clinging to floating wreckage.

Grace's brothers were away. Her father needed Grace to help with the rescue. The wreck was about three quarters of a mile from the lighthouse. It was almost impossible for just two people to row the small boat through the gigantic waves. But somehow they got to the wreck.

William jumped out on the rocks to help the people. Some of them were badly injured. Grace was left alone in the boat. She had to throw all her weight against the oars to keep the boat from crashing into the rocks as the steamer had done.

The rowboat was too small to carry everyone back to the lighthouse in one trip. Grace, her father, and three of the least-injured survivors rowed two of the worst wounded back through the storm. Grace stayed at the lighthouse to care for the injured. Her father and the other men rowed back for more survivors. Nine people were rescued that night.

Newspapers all over England praised Grace's heroism. Victoria, Queen of England, sent Grace a reward. The English people adored their brave young heroine. Stories, poems, and songs were written about her. Portraits were painted of her. Grace had so much attention she had a hard time keeping up with her daily work at the lighthouse.

Just four years later, Grace died of tuberculosis. The people mourned her passing. They built a statue so that no one would ever forget her courageous rescue effort that stormy night at sea.

One of the people inspired by Grace's heroism was an American named Ida Lewis. She was born on the day Grace died. Her father was Captain Hosea Lewis. He was keeper of the Lime Rock Lighthouse in Newport, Rhode Island. Like Grace, Ida lived in the lighthouse with her family. She helped tend the light.

When Ida was 16, her father had a bad stroke. She took over all of his duties. One of her first tasks was to rescue four men whose boat had capsized in Newport harbor. From that day on, Ida was fearless. She rowed alone through all kinds of weather to rescue sailors and would-be sailors from the sea. She just thought it was her job. She never thought of herself as unusual or even particularly brave.

The people who heard about her had other ideas. Many news stories were written about this amazing woman. One paper described her as "never weighing more than 103 pounds, even in the best condition, so that her endurance and strength are the more remarkable." She completed more than 18 rescues at sea during her lifetime. She kept the lighthouse up until her last rescue, when she was 64 years old.

She became known as the Heroine of Lime Rock. Hundreds of people sailed around the lighthouse just to catch a glimpse of her. Others sent gifts and letters to her. Her greatest gift was the Congressional Medal of Honor. She was the first woman to receive this prestigious medal.

Today, people still link her name with Grace Darling's when they remember some of the greatest sea rescues in history.

Activities

I. Recalling the Rescue

Answer the following questions to see how many details you can remember from the story.

1. What country was Grace Darling from?

2. How many children were in the Darling family?

3. How many rooms were in their lighthouse home?

4. How old was Grace when the steamship was wrecked on the rocks by her lighthouse?

5. How far was the wreck from the lighthouse?

6. How did Grace die?

7. How old was Ida when she took over her father's duties at the Lime Rock lighthouse?

8. Ida was the first woman in the United States to receive what medal?

II. *If You Had Been in This Situation . . .*

1. What would you have done if Grace's father had left you alone in the boat while he went ashore to rescue the survivors of the wreck?

2. What would you like best about living in a lighthouse? What would you like least about it?

3. What would you do if you suddenly found yourself in the spotlight for doing a brave deed?

III. Vocabulary to the Rescue

Locate the following words in the story. Make a new sentence about an amazing rescue adventure for each.

- daring

- weight

- oars

- violent

- drowned

- clinging

- wreckage

- storm

- wounded

- survivors

Priscilla the Pig

In many ways, Priscilla was not an ordinary pig. For one thing, she liked the water. She loved to swim. From her earliest days she'd been swimming in ponds by her home in San Marcos, Texas.

For another thing, Priscilla loved people. Her natural mother rejected her when she was born. So her owner, Ada, bottle-fed her. Ada decided it was easier to have Priscilla close by. So she kept the pig in a playpen on her front porch.

Priscilla liked all this special attention. It made her feel different from the other pigs on the farm. She was not interested in eating with the other pigs. Nor was she interested in playing with any of them. She did not even like to get dirty.

For Priscilla, a special treat was to go to Lake Somerville for a swim. She was invited to go one hot July afternoon when Carol and her 11-year-old son Anthony came to visit Ada. Carol was a good swimmer. Anthony, who was mentally handicapped, couldn't swim. But he loved to sit on the side of the lake with his feet in the water. He liked to watch Priscilla frolic about.

Priscilla had a harness with a long leash attached to it. Carol held the end of the leash and together they swam out to the center of the lake. Priscilla was a very good swimmer, even with her short legs.

The time came for one last swim. They hated to leave the cool water. But it was getting late. They did not want to get too tired before heading home.

Priscilla swam out in front. But she stopped when she heard Carol cry out. At first Priscilla thought her friend was in trouble. But it wasn't Carol. It was Anthony. He was walking into the lake toward them. Carol shouted for him to turn back. But Anthony kept right on walking out into the water.

He was smiling when he suddenly hit a deep spot and disappeared underwater. Carol dropped Priscilla's leash. She swam as fast as she could toward the spot where Anthony had gone down. Anthony's head bobbed above water only to sink again within seconds.

Meanwhile Priscilla had forgotten all about feeling tired. She, too, was swimming toward the spot. She was amazingly quick. She got there before Carol. Anthony bobbed up again, coughing and sputtering. He saw Priscilla. He reached out to grab her leash. He caught it. But in his frantic attempt, he pulled Priscilla down with him. The 22-pound pig was no match for an 11-year-old boy.

Priscilla knew they'd both drown if she didn't do something quick. She lunged for the surface. Both she and Anthony came up. This time Anthony was too tired to flail about. He let himself go limp. Priscilla struggled to tow him to shore. Fortunately Carol caught up with the exhausted pair and helped pull Anthony to safety.

It was an amazing rescue for a pig. The mayor named Saturday, August 25, 1984, Priscilla the Pig Day. He gave Priscilla a special medal. Many people came to the ceremony. Priscilla attended wearing a bikini and a purple cape. She was a very special pig indeed!

Activities

I. Recalling the Rescue

Answer the following questions to see how many details you remember from the story.

1. What was unique about Priscilla?

2. What was the name of Priscilla's adopted mother?

3. When Priscilla was a baby, what kept her on the front porch?

4. How did Carol hold on to Priscilla when they were swimming?

5. Was Anthony afraid of the water?

6. How much did Priscilla weigh when she rescued Anthony?

7. How did Priscilla try to get Anthony to shore?

8. What did Priscilla wear to her award ceremony?

II. If You Had Been in This Situation . . .

1. Would you have tried to keep Priscilla out of the water?

2. What would you do if you saw someone you knew could not swim slip underwater?

3. What kind of reward would you have given Priscilla?

III. *Vocabulary to the Rescue*

Locate each of the following words in the story. Make a new sentence about an amazing rescue adventure for each.

- ordinary

- rejected

- attention

- handicapped

- frolic

- leash

- bobbed

- sputtering

- flail

- underwater

Lifesaving Underwear

John Wesley Powell lost his right arm in 1862 in the Battle of Shiloh during the Civil War. But that loss didn't slow down this Yankee soldier. After the war ended, Powell became a naturalist and a geologist. He led many expeditions exploring the American West.

In 1869, the government asked Powell to make a geological survey of the Colorado River and its tributaries. He organized a team of nine explorers. Powell and his group were the first scientists to ride the Colorado River rapids through the Grand Canyon.

However, Powell almost didn't make it to the Grand Canyon. He nearly lost his life in Utah. Powell and expedition member George Bradley were scaling an 800-foot rock wall above the Green River. As they inched across the sheer wall, Powell spotted what looked like a good toehold. He made a jump for it.

The jump was successful. But when Powell looked around for the next toehold, there wasn't one. He couldn't go back. He couldn't go forward. Powell was trapped.

Bradley climbed to a ledge above Powell. But his arm couldn't quite reach the stranded explorer.

Foolishly, they weren't carrying any rope. No trees grew on the steep canyon wall. So Bradley couldn't extend a sturdy branch to his friend.

Bradley tried the long leather case that held the barometer the team carried for scientific observations. He pushed it out over the edge. He was careful not to loosen rocks that could start a landslide. He lowered one end down to Powell. It reached. But it was too thick and the leather was too slippery. Powell couldn't grasp it and hold it with his one hand.

Powell could feel his leg muscles trembling. Those muscles were straining to hold him up against the rock. If they gave out, he would plunge 800 feet down to certain death in the river below.

Bradley had to find something long enough to reach Powell. It had to be small enough to hold on to with one hand. It had to be strong enough to pull Powell up to safety.

Suddenly Bradley thought of his long johns. He yanked off his boots, shirt, and pants, and stripped on the spot. He twisted his underwear good and tight. Then he tossed one end over the ledge.

The long johns swung above Powell's head. To reach them, Powell had to let go of the wall. He knew he had just one chance. After he let go of the rock, there would be no second chance.

Time was up. His legs gave out. Powell made a lunge for the long johns. He caught the cloth in his hand. He held on for his life.

Bradley pulled steadily, hand over hand, until he got a good grip on Powell's arm. Then Bradley pulled him safely onto the ledge.

The team went on to successfully chart the Grand Canyon. In later years Powell became the director of the U.S. Geological Survey and of the Bureau of American Ethnology. Who knows what might have happened if Bradley had not worn his long johns for that fateful day of rock climbing above the Green River.

Activities

I. Recalling the Rescue

Answer the following questions to see how many details you can remember from the story.

1. In what Civil War battle did Powell lose his right arm?

2. What did Powell become after the war?

3. Where did he lead many expeditions?

4. What river was Powell surveying?

5. What part of the country was Powell in when he became trapped on the ledge?

6. What did Bradley first use to try to reach Powell?

7. What was the big risk when Powell reached for the long johns?

8. Later, Powell became director of what survey?

II. If You Had Been in This Situation . . .

1. If you had only one arm, would you try to scale rock walls?

2. If you had been Bradley, how would you have secured yourself so you wouldn't fall when you tried to pull Powell up from the ledge?

3. If you had been part of this near-tragic expedition, what would you be sure to remember on your next trek?

III. *Vocabulary to the Rescue*

Locate each of the following words in the story. Make a new sentence about an amazing rescue adventure for each.

- Yankee

- soldier

- expeditions

- exploring

- tributary

- scaling

- toehold

- ledge

- stranded

- geological

Faster Than a Speeding Bullet

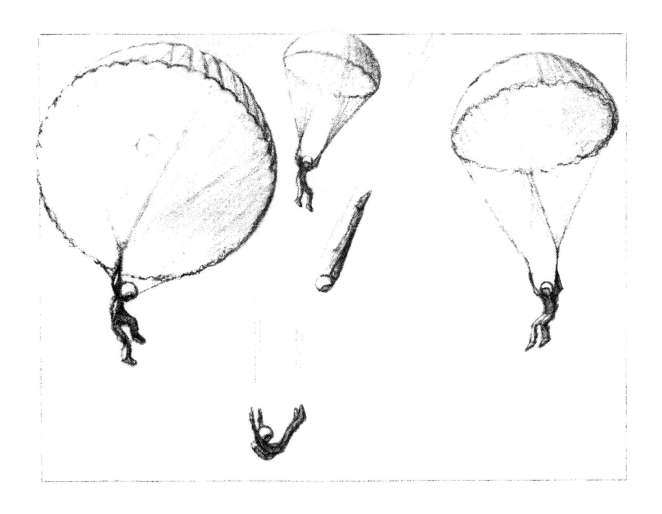

Debbie Williams had planned a great Easter weekend. She and her friends were going to a huge parachute convention. Over 420 jumpers would be meeting in Coolidge, Arizona.

Williams loved to skydive. This weekend she was planning to jump from an airplane with five of her friends. They were going to do a six-way circle.

The six-way circle was a difficult jump. The six skydivers had to work as a team. The first four jumped out of the plane together. They slowed the rate of their free-fall down to 120 mph by arching their backs, spreading their arms and legs, and bending their legs at the knees. The fifth jumper came down a little faster to catch up with the first four. The sixth jumper did a very fast free-fall to overtake the rest of the group.

Williams was scheduled to be the sixth jumper. She wasn't worried. She had 55 jumps in her skydiving career.

Everything was fine at first. The plane leveled off at 13,500 feet. Jump coordinator Greg Robertson gave the okay signal for the jump.

Then the trouble began. The first four jumpers couldn't hold the circle together. The fifth jumper, Guy Fitzwater, came down too fast. He knocked the other four out of control.

Williams was already streaking towards the group. Robertson was last out of the plane so that he could oversee the others. He saw that Williams was on a collision course with Fitzwater. Robertson tried to speed up his fall to help Williams. But he was too late.

Williams smashed headfirst right into Fitzwater. Luckily Fitzwater was only momentarily stunned. He was able to stabilize himself and open his parachute.

Williams was not so lucky. She was knocked unconscious. She was now plummeting towards the ground at 156 mph.

There was only one thing Robertson could do. He put himself into a steep dive. He aimed his head straight down, put his arms at his sides, and pointed his toes. That way he got as much speed out of the dive as possible. He was going 180 mph when he caught up to Williams.

She was out cold. Her face was covered with blood. Robertson had to pull Williams's ripcord hard enough to get her chute to open. They were just 2500 feet above the ground. In 15 seconds they would hit the earth. He *had* to get her chute open.

He yanked the cord as hard as he could. It popped open. Then he pulled open his own chute—not a second too soon—at 2000 feet above ground. He landed safely. Williams landed on her back. She was badly injured. Her skull was cracked. She had broken eight ribs and her collarbone. But she was alive.

Everyone treated Robertson like a hero. The President of the United States sent him a letter praising him for his bravery. People started calling him Superman. But Robertson did not want to be a hero. "I just want to be a skydiver," he said. He certainly was that and more on the day he saved Williams's life.

Activities

I. Recalling the Rescue

Answer the following questions to see how many details you remember about the story.

1. Where was the parachute convention?

2. How many jumpers planned to participate that weekend?

3. What special jump did Williams want to do with her friends?

4. How did the first jumpers slow their rate of falling?

5. How high was the plane before they started jumping?

6. How many jumpers went before Williams?

7. What was the name of the jumper Williams crashed into?

8. How fast did Robertson have to go to catch up to Williams?

II. *If You Had Been in This Situation . . .*

1. Would you ever go skydiving? Why or why not?

2. If you had been Fitzwater, would you have tried to help Williams before you opened your chute?

3. Do you think there would have been another way to get Williams safely to ground, if you could not have yanked her chute open?

III. *Vocabulary to the Rescue*

Locate each of the following words in the story. Make a new sentence about an amazing rescue adventure for each.

- parachute

- skydive

- airplane

- six-way circle

- free-fall

- collision

- smashed

- stabilize

- unconscious

- dive

Frozen Alive

One of the most bizarre sea stories happened off the coast of Maine. A winter storm raged over Rockland on the night of December 22, 1850. It was bitter cold. Violent winds blew snow and freezing rain over the seaport. Towering waves crashed onto the rocky coastline, leaving sheets of ice in their wake.

No one—not even Mainers, who are known for their fortitude on the sea—would have been foolhardy enough to attempt to sail out of port. In the harbor, Richard Ingraham, his fiancée Lydia Dyer, and their seaman Roger Elliot felt safe and dry aboard their schooner. They had taken extra care in securing their anchor line. Then they had gone belowdeck for the night. They slept peacefully, unaware of the growing intensity of the storm.

Near midnight the anchor rope snapped. The powerful storm swept the schooner up like a toy boat and hurled it out of the harbor. Surely it would have been lost in the raging sea if it hadn't crashed against the rocks by Owls Head point.

Jolted awake, the terrified passengers stumbled up on deck. Everything on the wrecked schooner was sheathed in a thick layer of ice. The wind and the waves rocked the boat so rakishly that it was impossible to stand. There was no way to signal for help. No one could see them through the blinding snow.

Ingraham made his way back down below to the cabin. He grabbed every blanket he could find and brought them all back up on deck. He wrapped his fiancée from head to foot. He helped her to lie down on the deck. Then he wrapped himself in a blanket and lay down on top of her. He told Elliott to do the same.

The huddled forms were quickly covered in a layer of ice. Elliot pulled out his knife. He chipped a hole in the ice so the three could breathe.

Hours later the storm finally began to let up. Elliot chipped his way out of their frozen cocoon. Ingraham and Dyer didn't move. Elliot was afraid they were dead.

Somehow, though nearly frozen through, Elliot made his way off the schooner. He climbed over the icy rocks until he found help. He told his rescuer that two others were still on the wreck. Then he passed out.

The rescue party found Ingraham and Dyer locked in a huge block of ice, frozen to the deck of the schooner. The rescuers sawed the block of ice away from the schooner's shattered deck. They coiled ropes around the ice block. Then they dragged it over the rocks to the point. There a driver was waiting with a wagon and team of horses. It took seven men to lift the block of ice on to the wagon.

The rescuers drove to a neighbor's house. Then they began the tortuously slow process of thawing the ice. They poured warm water over the ice to melt it. At the same time, they gently chipped away at the block, using hammers and small hand chisels.

At last the rescuers got down to the blankets. But they couldn't just peel them off. That might have torn the victims' skin. So they poured more warm water over the blankets. Finally they were able to ease the blankets away from the bodies.

Still, they could not tell if the couple were dead or alive. They first poured cold water over the bodies. Then they slowly increased the temperature of the water. They also rubbed the bodies to get the blood circulating.

The rescuers tried everything they could think of to revive the couple. Then, miraculously, Dyer opened her eyes. Before long, Ingraham also woke up, "What's all this?" he asked. "Where are we?"

It took many months for the couple to fully recover. But they did. Their time spent frozen alive had no long-lasting effects. They were married the next summer. They raised four children. They lived a full life.

Ironically, they fared much better than Elliot. The seaman never fully recovered from the frostbite and exhaustion he suffered in his amazing rescue effort.

Activities

I. Recalling the Rescue

Answer the following questions to see how many details you remember from the story.

1. In what part of Maine does this story take place?

2. In what century did this happen?

3. Why did the three sailors feel safe on board the schooner on the night of the storm?

4. About what time did the anchor line snap?

5. What prevented the schooner and all aboard from being washed out to sea?

6. What was Dyer's relationship to Ingraham?

7. How did the three manage to breathe under the ice?

8. What did the neighbors do to get Dyer's and Ingraham's frozen blood circulating again?

II. If You Had Been in This Situation . . .

1. Would you have stayed on board during the storm?

2. Would you have gone below deck to stay out of the storm after the schooner crashed on the rocks?

3. How would you have tried to defrost the block of ice around Dyer and Ingraham?

III. *Vocabulary to the Rescue*

Locate each of the following words in the story. Make a new sentence about an amazing rescue adventure for each.

- bitter

- freezing

- foolhardy

- chisels

- storm

- jolted

- rakishly

- cocoon

- revive

- frostbite